The Surname Redwood

Susan Morris &
Wendy Bosberry-Scott

ISBN: 154050090X
ISBN-13: 978-1540500908

The question of surnames, their origins, distribution and history, lies at the heart of genealogy as well as being fascinating in its own right.

In the 1980s and 1990s, long before many genealogical sources were even indexed, let alone online, our Surname Report service provided expert assessments of the origins, history and distribution of selected British surnames, using the sources available at the time.

Now, with so many more sources available, we believe that these reports retain their value as studies of individual surnames, and so we are gradually making the Debrett Surname Archive available online and in print for the first time. Some modern indexes have been consulted to refresh and update the reports.

Debrett Ancestry Research Ltd, PO Box 379,
Winchester SO23 9YQ
Tel: 01962 841904
Email: info@debrettancestry.co.uk
Website: www.debrettancestry.co.uk

CONTENTS

Overview

The use of surnames in England began in the Norman period, when surnames were not necessarily hereditary but usually a form of description. Some described the individual's trade or profession; others were nicknames; some gave the father's Christian name; others gave the individual's place of residence or origin.

Different surnames might be used in different documents, or more than one surname given in one document. Early descriptions were fairly elaborate and by the thirteenth and fourteenth centuries these were simpler, but still variable, and indeed the instability of surnames continued until well into the seventeenth century.

Although some Normans would already have had hereditary surnames on their arrival in Britain, the passing on of a surname from generation to generation only became customary in Britain gradually during the course of the thirteenth and fourteenth centuries. At the end of this period most of the population apparently had surnames.

Variations in the spelling of a family's surname continue to be found until the present century. Before this, as most people could not read or write, the parish clerk or other official would write down the name as they heard it.

There are four main groups of surnames:

> A – Local names, which describe a person by his place of residence or origin.
>
> B – Occupational names, which describe a person by his trade or profession.
>
> C – Surnames of relationship, which refer to the Christian name of the father or other important relative.
>
> D – Nicknames or sobriquets, coined to describe a person in terms of his appearance or character.

The name Redwood falls into Category A, which is by far the largest category. Local names can be subdivided further into those surnames which derive directly from an existing place-name, and those which derive from a topographical description which might not necessarily have become an established place-name, such as Greenwood, Marsh, Nash, *etc.*

Origins and early examples

The surname Redwood probably originates from the place-name Redeswood in Northumberland.

Allen Mawer's *Place-Names of Northumberland and Durham* (Cambridge University Press, 1920) suggests that the origin of the place-name is 'Rede-wood', meaning (wood) 'by the river Rede'. The intrusion of the possessive 's' may be due to imitation of the neighbouring names Reedsmouth and Redesdale. The place-name appears in Assize Rolls of 1255 as *Redewode* and *Rodewode*. Mawer cites no other medieval examples but by 1663 the place-name appears as *Reedswood* in a rental.

The earliest example of the surname that has been found clearly links up with the surviving place-name: Reaney and Wilson's *Dictionary of English Surnames*, which is the authoritative modern source, cites the following name from the *Liber Feodorum* (Book of Fees) for Northumberland:

John de Redewod   Northumberland - *Liber Feodorum* 1242

John might have actually held the manor of Redeswood; or he might have simply lived there, or moved from there to somewhere else. Local surnames were usually preceded by a preposition such as *de*, *in*, or *at*: these prepositions were gradually dropped and by the end of the fourteenth century few were still in use.

No other medieval example of the surname has been found and Reaney and Wilson's other references come from the sixteenth and seventeenth centuries, many miles from Northumberland:

Nicholas Redewood	Essex	Feet of Fines 1527
John Redwood	Devon	Protestation Returns 1642

The name evidently remained in Northumberland, however, for the Mormon *International Genealogical Index* (1992, now superseded by *FamilySearch*) shows a marriage in 1592 (as well as a nineteenth-century reference from Newcastle):

Henry Reedwood	Berwick upon Tweed Marriage Register 1592

Northumberland is a long way from Devon. Although medieval society was more mobile than is sometimes thought, the possibility must therefore be considered that there were other Redwood place-names or topographical descriptions elsewhere in the country, now lost, which might have independently given rise to the surname.

Hanks & Hodges' *Dictionary of Surnames* (Oxford University Press, 1988) gives a hypothetical explanation of a lost place-name 'Redwood' deriving from the Old English words *read*, meaning red and *wuda*, meaning wood, suggesting that 'the reference is probably to birch trees as they appear in the spring'.

Distribution

In 1890 H B Guppy published his *Homes of Family Names in Great Britain*, still the only published work on surname distribution in Britain as a whole. His work was based on printed genealogies and a survey of county directories for the 1880s, in which he looked especially at the names of farmers, reasoning that they were among the most stable groups in society. Redwood did not appear in sufficient numbers to be included in this survey.

A survey of a cross section of parish registers for the years 1601 and 1602 was carried out in 1910 by F K and S Hitching; incidences of a particular surname are noted by parish and county, although with no indication of numbers of references. There were no entries for the name Redwood, again indicating relative rarity.

A useful guide to the distribution of surnames for the sixteenth, seventeenth and eighteenth centuries in England is provided by the indexes to wills proved, and administrations granted, at the Prerogative Court of (the Archbishop of) Canterbury, in London, which had superior jurisdiction over local ecclesiastical courts where wills were proved until 1858. The PCC thus provides a national index, although it is not a completely representative one, as testators whose wills were proved in the PCC were mostly among the wealthier members of society, and a disproportionate number of them were from London or Middlesex.

A search of the indexes for the years 1584 to 1800 found the following entries for Redwood:

1558-1599

1573   John Redwood, Reedwood, Redewood, the elder, St Stevens, Hertfordshire
1575   Edward Redwood, Charde Borough, Somerset
1586   John Redwood, Seaton, Devon
1597   John Redwood, Colney Street, St Albans, Hertfordshire

Seventeenth Century

1604   John Redwood, gent., London, par. of St Stephens near the town of St Albans, Hertfordshire
1613   Thomas Redwood, mariner, precinct of the Tower of London
1614   Agnes Redwood, widow, Liberty of the Tower of London
1615   Katherine Redwood, wife of Robert Redwood, gent., Bristol, Gloucs.
1625   William Redwood, gunner of the ship 'Abigaile'
1653/4 Margarett Redwood, spinster, St Margaretts, Canterbury, Kent
1656   Francis Redwood, yeoman, Aldenham, Hertfordshire
1659   John Redwood, yeoman, Auliscombe, Devon
1659   Mary Redwood, widow, St Buttolphe, Bishopsgate, London
1660   John Redwood, gent, Seaton, Rut.; late of St Dunstans in the West, London
1668   John Redwood, Wapping (St Mar Whitechapel) Middx, mariner
1669   John Redwood, St Dunstan West, London
1669   Nicholas Redwood, iremonger, Exeter
1669   William Redwood, the elder, feltmaker, Bristol
1675   Nicholas Redwood, City of Exeter

1688   Thomas Redwood, yeoman, Aldenham,
        Hertfordshire

Eighteenth Century
1751   Richard Redwood, Kent
1754   Thomas Redwood, Kent
1766   Isaac Redwood, Middlesex
1776   Jeremiah Redwood Esq., Kent
1785   Sarah Redwood, Kent
1789   Abraham Redwood, *Pts*
1790   William Redwood, *Pts*, no ship
1795   Henry Redwood, London
1799   Robert Redwood, Middlesex

1800-1857
1800   Richard Redwood, gardener and hawker of
        Islington, Middlesex
1804   Mary Redwood of St Leonard Shoreditch,
        Middlesex
1805   Francis Christopher Redwood, pay master in
        HM fifth regiment of Dragoon Guards
1807   Jonas Langford Redwood of St Marylebone,
        Middlesex
1808   Jeremiah Redwood, of Lyme Regis, Dorset
1814   Adam Redwood, husbandman of St Stephen,
        Hertfordshire
1817   Mary Redwood, widow of Wellington,
        Somerset
1823   Mary Ann Redwood of Wellington, Somerset
1826   Abraham Redwood of Queen Ann Street East,
        Middlesex
1834   Potter Jeremiah Redwood of Lyme Regis,
        Dorset
1835   Edward Redwood of the London Life
        Assurance Office, Canon Street, Middlesex
1838   Abraham Redwood of St Marylebone,
        Middlesex
1842   William Redwood, labourer of Chislet, Kent

1844   Langford Redwood of Flushing, Queens, New York, USA

1847   Thomas Redwood, deputy storekeeper of HM Ordnance of Simons Town, Cape of Good Hope

1857   Ann Redwood, widow of Peckham, Surrey

The PCC was the usual court used for testators who died abroad and although there are four mariners in this list, only two are marked as dying 'in foreign parts' (*Pts*).

When the London and Middlesex examples, and those who died abroad, are taken out of the picture, we are left with what is probably a single family group near St Alban's, Hertfordshire in the sixteenth and seventeenth centuries; and at the same time another more widespread group in the west country (Bristol, Devon and Somerset). Reaney and Wilson's example from the Protestation Returns of 1642 (see above), fits into this group. By the eighteenth century a third group has emerged in Kent (the earliest Kent example being however from the previous century) and the Hertfordshire and West Country groups have disappeared from the picture (although the west country group at least was certainly still there a century later: see below).

The absence of Northumberland entries from this list is not really surprising. It was a long journey from Northumberland to London to prove a will and wealthier testators would have favoured the Prerogative Court of York.

The West Country examples noted above can probably be accounted for by the family of the Baronets Redwood.

8

This baronetcy was granted relatively recently in 1911 but the family can trace their ancestry back to Colyton, South Devon, in the early part of the sixteenth century. Their entry in *Burke's Peerage and Baronetage* (1970) shows how the family extended into Bristol, Somerset and Glamorganshire. Their influence also spread abroad: Abraham Redwood, son of another Abraham who was a ship's master in the West Indies, founded the Redwood library in Newport, Rhode Island in 1747.

Dr Theophilus Redwood (1806-1892), father of the first Baronet, was an eminent pharmacist. His son, Sir Thomas Boverton Redwood (1846-1911), achieved equal eminence in the field of chemistry for his work on petroleum. He died only months after the creation of the title.

For the nineteenth century, H B Guppy's survey has been mentioned above. Another important Victorian source is the *Return of Owners of Land* of 1873, sometimes known as the Modern Domesday Book. This source lists, county by county, every owner of an acre of land or more, with their residence (not necessarily the address of their property) and the acreage of their holding.

Return of Owners of Land

Devon	2	Redwood
Glamorgan	3	Redwood
Kent	1	Redwood
Monmouth	1	Redwood
Somerset	3	Redwood
Somerset	1	Ridwood
Southampton	1	Redwards

The Devon, Glamorgan and Somerset references may refer to the family of the Baronets Redwood.

Two variations of the name have appeared in this list: Ridwood in Somerset and Redwards in Hampshire (formerly the county of Southampton).

The first decennial census return in England, Scotland and Wales was taken in 1801, but personal information was only recorded from 1841 onwards. From 1851, the age, occupation and birthplace is given for each member of the household, and so these records provide invaluable genealogical information as well as a fascinating 'snapshot' of the family in the nineteenth century. The latest return currently open to public inspection is that of 1911 and there are now national indexes to the returns from 1841 onwards, although these indexes are not wholly reliable. Using these indexes, we found the following numbers for Redwood, Reedwood and Redewood in England, Scotland and Wales:

6 June 1841
Redwood (455); Reedwood (1); Redewood (3)

30 March 1851
Redwood (532); Redewood (3)

7 April 1861
Redwood (572); Reedwood (1); Redewood (1)

2 April 1871
Redwood (689); Reedwood (7); Redewood (13)

3 April 1881
Redwood (751); Reedwood (7); Redewood (1)

5 April 1891
Redwood (891); Reedwood (8); Redewood (11)

31 March 1901
Redwood (1005); Reedwood (5); Redewood (8)

2 April 1911
Redwood (1075); Reedwood (4); Redewood (1)

Redwood is the dominant form, as expected, but still only shows relatively low numbers, indicating its relative rarity as a surname. Very few entries were indexed for the variants Reedwood and Redewood with the last-mentioned barely reaching double figures in 1871 and 1891.

Arms

Dr Theophilus Redwood and Lewis Redwood were granted arms, for which the emblazon is shown in Burke's *General Armory* (1884) as follows:

> **Redwood** (Boverton, co. Glamorgan; granted to Theophilus Redwood, Ph.D., of London, and Rhymney, co. Monmouth, and Lewis Redwood, Surgeon, of Orchard House, Boverton). Paly of six or and ermines a lion rampant sable on a chief azure an embattled gateway proper between two mullets of six points of the first.
>
> *Crest* - A rock, therefrom an eagle rising proper charged on each wing with a mullet of six points or, in the beak a staff raguly gold.
>
> *Motto* - Lumen servimus antique.

Printed Genealogies

The following works deal with the family of the Baronets Redwood:

Burke's *Landed Gentry* (1858)
Burke's *Peerage and Baronetage* 1970
V L Oliver, *The History of the Island of Antigua*, (1894-1899), iii, 44

Summary

To conclude, the name Redwood originates from the place-name Redeswood in Northumberland, and probably also from a similar place-name or place-names elsewhere, now lost to us. It is a relatively rare name in national terms although certain groupings can be identified, in the West Country, in Hertfordshire in the sixteenth and seventeenth centuries, and in Kent.

Sources Consulted

Allen Mawer, *Place-Names of Northumberland and Durham* (Cambridge University Press, 1920)

P H Reaney, *The Origins of English Surnames* (London: Routledge & Kegan Paul, 1967)

P H Reaney & R M Wilson, *A Dictionary of British Surnames* (Oxford: Oxford University Press, 3rd edition, 1995)

P H Reaney, *Dictionary of British Surnames* (London: Routledge & Kegan Paul, 2nd edition, 1976)

P Hanks & F Hodges, *A Dictionary of Surnames* (Oxford University Press, 1988)

M A Lower, *Patronymica Brittanica* (London, 1860)

C W Bardsley, *Dictionary of English and Welsh Surnames* (1901: reprinted, Baltimore: Genealogical Publishing Co, 1967)

C L'Estrange Ewen, *Guide to the Origin of British Surnames* (London: John Gifford, 1938)

H B Guppy, *Homes of Family Names in Great Britain* (London, 1890)

Ernest Weekley, *The Romance of Names* (London: John Murray, 2nd edition, 1917)

Ernest Weekley, *Surnames* (London: John Murray, 1917)

George F Black, *The Surnames of Scotland* (New York Public Library, 1946)

Edward McLysaght, *The Surnames of Ireland* (Dublin: Irish University Press, 1977)

T J & Prys Morgan, *Welsh Surnames* (Cardiff: University of Wales Press, 1985)

F K & S Hitching, *References to English Surnames in 1601* (Walton on Thames: Bernau, 1910)

F K & S Hitching, *References to English Surnames in 1602* (Walton on Thames: Bernau, 1911)

Debrett's People of Today (Debrett's Peerage Limited: London, 1996)

The Dictionary of National Biography: Index & Epitome (London, 1906)

The Concise Dictionary of National Biography, Part II, 1901–1950, (Oxford, 1961)

Burke's Family Index (London: Burke's Peerage Limited, 1976)

H R Moulton, *Palaeography, Genealogy & Topography* (Sale Catalogue, 1930)

Index to Prerogative Court of Canterbury Wills (The National Archives: online)

G W Marshall, *The Genealogist's Guide* (1903; reprinted, Baltimore: GPC 1973)

J B Whitmore, *A Genealogical Guide* (London, 1953)

Charles Bridge, *An Index to Pedigrees* (London, 1867)

Geoffrey B Barrow, *The Genealogist's Guide* (London: Research Publishing Co, 1977)

Sir Bernard Burke, *The General Armory* (London, 1884)

C R Humphrey-Smith, editor, *Burke's General Armory Volume II*, (Tabard Press, 1973)

The Return of Owners of Land (1873)

Eilert Ekwall, *The Concise Oxford Dictionary of English Place-Names* (Oxford: Clarendon Press, 4th edition, 1960)

E G Withycombe, *The Oxford Dictionary of English Christian Names* (Oxford: Clarendon Press, 2nd edition, 1950)

W J Hardy & W Page, *A Calendar to the Feet of Fines for London and Middlesex: Vol 1 Richard I – Richard III (1189–1485)* (London, 1892)

Richard McKinley, *The Surnames of Oxfordshire* (English Surnames Series III: Leopard's Head Press, 1977)

Richard McKinley, *The Surnames of Sussex* (English Surnames Series V: Leopard's Head Press, 1988)

Richard McKinley, *The Surnames of Lancashire* (English Surnames Series IV: Leopard's Head Press, 1981)

Richard McKinley, *Norfolk and Suffolk Surnames in the Middle Ages* (English Surnames Series II: Phillimore, 1975)

George Redmonds, *Yorkshire West Riding* (English Surnames Series I: Phillimore, 1973)

Mr Avenell, *The Norman People* (London, 1874)

Debrett's Heraldry (London, 1933)

J P Brooke-Little, revised, *Boutell's Heraldry* (Frederick Warne: London, 1970)

Indexes to 1841–1911 Census Returns of England and Wales (The National Archives/*Ancestry.com*)

www.ingramcontent.com/pod-product-compliance
Lightning Source LLC
Chambersburg PA
CBHW070255290526
45789CB00004B/1857